SHARP MINDS
Learning

I0099382

AMAZING STORIES FOR SHARP MINDS

True Tales of Discovery, Curiosity, and Courage.

ALI HASSAN

ISBN: 978-1-7395118-6-9

How to Read This Book

(A Small Guide for Curious Minds)

There's no wrong way to explore "Amazing Stories For Sharp Minds."

This isn't a book you have to read in order — it's a collection of true stories, each one a spark of discovery. You can start anywhere that catches your eye.

Here are a few ways to make the most of your journey:

- ● Choose your path. Flip through the Table of Contents and pick a story that calls to you — a scientist, an animal, a mystery, or a spark of light.

- 🔍 Look for patterns. Notice how curiosity connects them all. Every story starts with a question, but ends with something beautiful and creative.

- ✏️ Pause and wonder. After each story, take a moment to think. What would you have done? What new question does it make you want to ask?

- 🎭 Imagine the scene. Use the illustrations as windows — imagine what it smelled like, sounded like, or felt like to be there.

- 💡 Share the light. Tell someone what amazed you. Curiosity grows when it's shared.

You don't need a lab coat or a map to begin — only an open heart and a curious mind.

So turn the page, adventurer.

Let's discover how truth can be even more magical than fiction.

TABLE OF CONTENTS

INTRODUCTION

Have you ever heard a story so weird you thought, "That can't be true!"

Well... surprise! Sometimes the strangest stories are the real ones.

This book is full of true tales — about clever kids, wacky animals, brave heroes, and lucky accidents that changed the world. You'll meet the girl who named Pluto over breakfast, the librarian who measured the Earth with a stick, the human computers who launched rockets to the Moon, and the shrimp that punches faster than a bullet. You'll discover octopuses carrying coconut armour, fish that walk on land, trees that whisper underground, and a desert that blooms overnight.

Some stories will make you laugh. Others might make you say "wow!" or even "eww!" But each one will show you how wonderfully odd, funny, and fascinating our world can be.

Humans are pretty weird, too. We've made mistakes that turned into brilliant ideas, fought battles against nature, and sent messages through space. Sometimes we save the planet. Sometimes we nearly destroy it. But we always keep trying — and that's where the best stories begin.

Animals have their own kind of genius. Some build houses underwater. Some talk with colours or music. Some are just plain bizarre — like frogs that freeze solid all winter and then hop away in spring. You'll see how nature is full of surprises if you look closely enough.

Every story in this book really happened. The people were real, the places exist, and the facts have been checked (even the silly ones!).

So grab a snack, get comfy, and prepare to travel through time, space, and imagination — no spaceship required.

When you're done, you might start seeing your own life a little differently. Because sometimes, the next amazing true story is waiting to happen to you.

Ready? You can just turn the page and start your adventure.

Truth is about to get a lot more exciting.

New Planet
Discovered!

The Girl Who Named Pluto

In 1930, astronomers made an incredible discovery — a tiny, frozen world at the edge of our solar system. It was smaller than any known planet, and so far away that even the most powerful telescopes could barely see it.

The discovery made headlines around the world. Newspapers called it "a mysterious new planet beyond Neptune." But there was one big question no one could answer yet:

"What should we name it?"

Letters poured in from every corner of the globe. People suggested names from ancient myths, famous explorers, and even pets! But none of them seemed quite right.

Meanwhile, across the ocean in Oxford, England, an 11-year-old girl named Venetia Burney sat at the breakfast table with her family. Venetia was curious and bright. She loved books about space, stars, and mythology, and her home was full of stories thanks to her grandfather, Falconer Madan, a retired librarian from Oxford University.

That morning, as sunlight streamed through the window, her grandfather looked up from the newspaper and said,

"Venetia, they've discovered a new planet — but it doesn't have a name yet."

Venetia paused, her spoon still in her hand. She thought about this cold, distant world spinning in the dark. Then she said thoughtfully,

"Why not call it Pluto?"

Her grandfather looked surprised. "Pluto? That's an interesting name. Why?"

Venetia smiled and explained, "In Roman mythology, Pluto is the god of the underworld. He lives in a cold, dark place — far from the light of the Sun. That sounds just like this new planet."

Her grandfather was impressed. It was a clever, meaningful name — mysterious, short, and powerful. So he decided to tell someone who could make a difference.

That same morning, he wrote a letter to his friend Herbert Hall Turner, a well-known astronomer at Oxford. Turner liked the name too, and he quickly sent it across the Atlantic Ocean to the Lowell Observatory in Flagstaff, Arizona, USA, where the new planet had been discovered.

At the observatory, scientists had already received hundreds of suggestions. But when they saw "Pluto," something clicked. The name fit perfectly. It belonged to a mythological god, just like the other planets.

On March 24, 1930, the scientists voted. Every single one of them chose Pluto.

A few weeks later, the world heard the exciting announcement:

"The new planet will be called Pluto."

Venetia's idea had travelled thousands of miles, crossed an ocean, and captured the imagination of scientists and dreamers everywhere. Newspapers wrote stories about "the little girl who named a planet," and Venetia became an overnight celebrity. She received letters from all over the world — from scientists, teachers, and children who admired her creativity.

MORAL OF THE STORY

You don't have to be a grown-up to make a big discovery. Curiosity, imagination, and courage can change the world — or even name a planet! So keep wondering, keep learning, and never be afraid to share your ideas. You never know how far they might travel — maybe even all the way to the stars. ✹

The Librarian Who Measured the Earth

Over two thousand years ago, in the golden city of Alexandria, the greatest library on Earth stood by the shining sea. Its tall marble columns and endless rows of scrolls were home to knowledge from every corner of the ancient world. Inside worked a man named Eratosthenes — a thinker, teacher, and dreamer.

He wasn't just any librarian. He was called "Beta" by his friends — not because he was second-best, but because he was good at everything. He studied math, poetry, geography, astronomy, and even music. But one question kept him awake at night:

"How big is the Earth?"

In those days, no one truly knew. Some thought the Earth might stretch on forever. Others believed it was round but couldn't say how round. There were no satellites, no aeroplanes, not even maps of the whole world. Just sailors, stars, and guesses.

One hot afternoon, Eratosthenes was reading a scroll when he came across something curious.

It said that in the city of Syene, far to the south, there was a deep well where, on the longest day of the year — the summer solstice — the sun shone straight down. The sunlight touched the bottom of the well, and tall pillars cast no shadow at all.

Eratosthenes blinked. "No shadow?" he thought. "Then the sun must be directly overhead in Syene."

But in Alexandria, where he lived, he had noticed that the sun did cast a shadow at the very same time of year. That could only mean one thing — the Earth's surface was curved.

That tiny difference in shadow gave him a brilliant idea.

If he could measure the angle of the shadow in Alexandria, and if he knew the distance between the two cities, he could figure out how big the entire planet was.

So on the next summer solstice, Eratosthenes set up a tall stick in the ground and waited for the midday sun. When the shadow reached its shortest point, he measured the angle — about seven degrees. Then, using reports from camel traders and travellers, he estimated the distance from Alexandria to Syene: roughly 5,000 stadia, or about 800 kilometres.

Now came the fun part — the math!

He realised that seven degrees was about one-fiftieth of a full circle.

So if 800 kilometres represented one-fiftieth of the Earth's circumference, then the entire Earth must be 800 × 50 = 40,000 kilometres around.

It was a number so big it amazed everyone who heard it. And the most incredible thing? He was almost exactly right.

With no satellites, no aeroplanes, and no GPS, one man had measured the size of the world — using nothing but sunlight, a stick, and his mind.

Eratosthenes became known as the Father of Geography. He drew maps showing the shape of continents and oceans, and he invented the first lines of latitude and longitude, which we still use today.

When people asked how he had done it, he just smiled and said,

"By letting the sun be my ruler."

MORAL OF THE STORY

Big discoveries don't always need big tools. Sometimes, the brightest ideas come from simple questions, careful thinking, and the courage to wonder, "What if...?" ✸

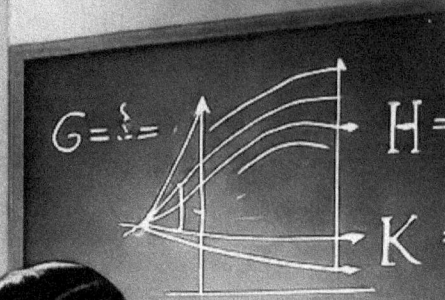

The Human Computers Who Sent Us to Space

Long before computers had screens or keyboards, there were people who were computers. They didn't beep or buzz—they thought. They calculated. They solved problems that would one day help humanity reach the stars.

In the 1940s and 1950s, during a time when most people thought math and science were "men's jobs," a group of brilliant women worked at the Langley Research Centre in Virginia, USA. They were called the "human computers."

Their job was to calculate flight paths, test data, and complex equations by hand—using pencils, rulers, and their incredible brains. Aeroplanes and rockets couldn't fly safely without their numbers. And when America decided to send astronauts into space, these women became the invisible force that made it possible.

One of them was Katherine Johnson. From the time she was a little girl in West Virginia, Katherine loved numbers more than anything. She counted everything—steps, stars, even the dishes she washed. By age 10, she was already in high school; by 18, she was a college graduate.

When she joined NASA's Space Task Group in 1958, the world was in the middle of the Space Race. The United States and the Soviet Union were competing to be the first to send humans beyond Earth. Astronauts depended on engineers to guide their ships — but behind those engineers were women like Katherine, who did the math no one else could.

One mission changed everything. In 1962, astronaut John Glenn was preparing to become the first American to orbit the Earth. The flight would be dangerous. The new electronic computers had checked the flight path, but Glenn didn't trust them completely.

Before liftoff, he said,

"Get the girl — the one who checked the numbers. If she says they're good, I'm ready to go."

"The girl" was Katherine Johnson. She spent hours reviewing every equation by hand, using only her calculator, pencils, and paper. When she confirmed the numbers matched, John Glenn launched — and made history safely.

At the same time, other remarkable women were also changing history.

Dorothy Vaughan became one of NASA's first Black supervisors and trained herself — and her team — to program the new IBM computers, ensuring they wouldn't be left behind.

Mary Jackson, another talented engineer, broke barriers by becoming NASA's first Black female aerospace engineer, helping design safer spacecraft.

These women faced both sexism and racism. They were often made to work in separate offices, use different bathrooms, and fight for the respect they deserved. But they didn't stop. Their work proved that genius has no colour and no gender — only courage and curiosity.

Because of them, astronauts made it into space, and humans set foot on the Moon. Decades later, the world finally began to recognise their incredible contributions. Their story inspired the award-winning book and film "Hidden Figures."

Today, young scientists everywhere can look up at the night sky and remember that before computers guided rockets, human minds did. And they did it with pencils, paper, and perseverance.

MORAL OF THE STORY

Courage, teamwork, and determination can break barriers — and even launch you beyond the stars. 🚀

The Kite Experiment That Caught Lightning

One summer evening in 1752, the sky above Philadelphia grew dark and heavy. The wind began to twist and roar, carrying the smell of rain. Most people hurried home, slamming shutters and latching doors. But one man and his young son went the opposite way — out into the storm.

The man was Benjamin Franklin — printer, inventor, scientist, and lover of experiments. He had studied lightning for years, wondering what it really was. People said it was fire from the gods or mysterious magic from the heavens. Franklin suspected otherwise. He believed lightning was a form of electricity, the same invisible energy that made sparks jump from his machines in the lab.

But how could he prove it?

He had a daring idea — one that sounded completely mad. He would fly a kite in a thunderstorm and try to capture the lightning itself!

So one evening, as the storm clouds rolled in, Franklin and his son William went to a nearby field.

21

They carried a simple kite made of silk, a wooden cross, and a thin metal wire at the top to attract an electric charge. The kite string was ordinary twine — except for one clever addition: at the end of it, Franklin tied a small metal key.

"Ready, son?" Franklin asked.

William nodded, gripping the spool as the wind tugged at the kite.

They released it into the sky. The wind howled. Thunder cracked. Rain began to fall. The kite danced wildly among the dark clouds, barely visible against flashes of light. Franklin sheltered under a small barn, watching closely.

At first, nothing happened. The string hung limp and wet. But then Franklin noticed something strange: the loose threads of the string began to stand upright, almost as if alive. He reached out his hand and felt a faint tingle.

Electricity!

He moved his knuckle close to the key, and a tiny blue spark jumped between them — a spark from the sky itself.

Franklin grinned, his hair damp and wild. "The lightning," he whispered, "is electric!"

He had just proved one of the greatest scientific discoveries of the age.

His experiment showed that lightning and electricity were the same — powerful natural forces, not magic.

From that moment on, Franklin became famous not just as an inventor but as a pioneer of understanding nature's hidden laws. He went on to create the lightning rod—a simple metal pole that protected buildings from fires during storms, saving countless lives and homes.

It's hard to imagine today, but back then, no one knew what electricity truly was. Franklin's daring curiosity turned danger into discovery — and forever changed how we understand the world.

MORAL OF THE STORY

Bravery and curiosity can light up the darkest storm — but true genius also knows when to stay safe. ⚡

24

The Artist Who Taught Math to Art

Imagine walking into a cathedral so tall that your neck aches looking up, or standing before a painting that feels so real, you could step right into it. Long before cameras or computers, one man discovered how to make drawings look three-dimensional — using nothing more than a pencil, a pane of glass, and mathematics.

His name was Leonardo da Vinci, and he lived in Italy more than 500 years ago, during a time called the Renaissance— when art, science, and invention came together like never before.

Even as a boy, Leonardo loved to draw. He filled notebooks with sketches of birds, people, machines, and the movement of water. But as he grew older, he began to ask questions most artists never thought about.

"Why do things far away look smaller?"

"How do shadows really fall?"

"Can art follow the same rules as nature?"

While other artists copied what they saw, Leonardo studied how seeing worked. He watched the way light hit walls and how buildings shrank in the distance. He realised there were mathematical rules behind what the eye saw — and he set out to understand them.

This idea — that you could draw space using geometry — was called perspective. Artists before him had guessed at it, but Leonardo mastered it. Using rulers, mirrors, and careful measurements, he discovered that all lines in a picture seem to meet at a single point in the distance — called the vanishing point.

When he applied this to his art, his paintings came alive. In works like The Last Supper, the walls and ceiling lines draw your eyes straight to the centre of the scene — making you feel like you're standing inside the room with Jesus and his disciples.

But Leonardo wasn't satisfied with just painting. He wanted to know everything.

He studied how the human body was built, dissecting muscles and bones to understand their forms. He sketched flying machines centuries before aeroplanes existed, and designed bridges, submarines, and even robots!

In Leonardo's notebooks — thousands of pages long — art and math danced together. Curving lines became equations, angles became beauty. He believed that math wasn't separate from art; it was its secret language.

"Learn how to see," he wrote. "Realise that everything connects to everything else."

Though Leonardo never published his scientific notes, his discoveries changed the world. Artists began using perspective and proportion to bring depth and realism to their work. Engineers, architects, and even game designers today still use the principles he uncovered centuries ago.

He proved that imagination and logic could work hand in hand — and that beauty could be measured, not to limit it, but to understand it.

MORAL OF THE STORY

Art and science aren't opposites—they're teammates. Curiosity can make creativity sharper, and beauty brighter. 🖌️✦

The Code Breakers with Paper and Pencils

During World War II, when battles were fought across land, sea, and sky, another kind of war was happening in secret — a war of numbers, letters, and logic.

Hidden inside a quiet country mansion in Bletchley Park, England, a group of the world's cleverest minds was racing against time. Their mission: to break a German code machine called the Enigma — a device that scrambled messages so completely that it seemed unbreakable.

Every day, German forces sent thousands of encrypted messages — orders, troop movements, and plans — all locked behind Enigma's spinning wheels and blinking lights. Without the code, the Allies couldn't read them. And if they couldn't read them, they couldn't win.

Inside Bletchley Park, mathematicians, linguists, and puzzle lovers sat hunched over long tables, surrounded by typewriters, notes, and machines. There were no computers like today — only pencils, papers, and brilliant human minds.

One of those minds belonged to a young mathematician named Alan Turing. He was shy, brilliant, and endlessly curious about patterns. He once said,

"Sometimes it's the people no one imagines anything of who do the things no one can imagine."

Alan realised that no human could solve Enigma's code fast enough — the settings changed every single day, creating billions of possible combinations. So he decided to invent a machine that could think faster than any person.

He called it the Bombe. It was a strange-looking device — filled with wheels, switches, and clicking parts — but it could test thousands of Enigma settings in minutes.

Day and night, the team worked in secret. The rooms buzzed with the sound of paper shuffling and machines humming. Sometimes they went without sleep for days, drinking tea by the gallon. They weren't soldiers with guns, but every message they decoded saved lives.

One cold morning, the Bombe clicked into silence. They had found it — the key to that day's Enigma setting! Within minutes, they could read enemy plans that had been invisible only hours before.

Alan's invention and the teamwork of hundreds of codebreakers changed the course of history. The messages they decoded helped the Allies win key battles — including the one that turned the tide of the war.

Yet their work was so secret that no one outside Bletchley Park knew. For decades, the story stayed hidden. The codebreakers couldn't tell their families or friends what they had done.

When the truth finally came out years later, people around the world were amazed. Historians estimated that their work shortened the war by at least two years and saved millions of lives.

Alan Turing didn't just help end the war — his ideas became the foundation for modern computers. Every time you use a smartphone, play a game, or send a message, you're using the legacy of his genius.

From paper and pencils to digital brains, it all began with a quiet man who believed that patterns could change the world.

MORAL OF THE STORY

Brains can be as powerful as armies. Even in dark times, intelligence, teamwork, and creativity can turn the tide. ●
✦

The Girl Who Made Plastic Disappear

Plastic is one of humanity's most useful inventions — and one of its biggest problems.

It's in everything we touch: water bottles, shopping bags, toothbrushes, and toys. But once we throw it away, it doesn't just vanish. It lingers for hundreds of years, breaking down into smaller and smaller pieces that float through oceans, rivers, and soil.

For most people, this seems too big a problem to fix. But two teenage girls from Vancouver, Canada — Miranda Wang and Jeanny Yao — decided they wouldn't just worry about it. They would do something.

It all began in 2012, when they were both high school students. During a science class trip to the Fraser River, they saw plastic waste tangled in reeds and floating among the driftwood. Bags, bottles, and wrappers were everywhere.

Jeanny frowned. "Why can't the Earth break this down like it does with everything else?" she asked.

That question stuck with Miranda. She knew that nature had bacteria that could decompose almost anything — fallen leaves, old food, even oil spills. But plastic? That was something bacteria had never evolved to eat.

Miranda wondered, What if we could help them learn?

Back at school, the two friends turned their question into an experiment. They began collecting samples of soil and water from different parts of their city—places polluted with plastic. Then, in their tiny school lab, they grew bacteria from those samples on dishes containing plastic materials.

It wasn't easy. They didn't have expensive lab equipment or research funding — just curiosity, determination, and a few microscopes. For weeks, nothing seemed to happen.

Then one afternoon, Jeanny peered into a dish and gasped. "Look at this!" she whispered.

Under the microscope, they saw tiny bacterial colonies forming around a piece of plastic. When they checked later, parts of the plastic had actually begun to break down.

They had found a kind of bacteria that could slowly eat plastic!

Their discovery was one of the first of its kind made by students. Soon, universities and environmental scientists took notice.

The girls presented their findings at international science fairs, inspiring other young researchers to look for biological solutions to pollution.

But Miranda and Jeanny didn't stop there. They grew up, went to university, and turned their school project into a full-fledged scientific mission. Together, they founded a company called BioCellection — now known as Novoloop — to develop technology that turns plastic waste into useful new materials like clothing fibres, running shoes, and car parts.

Instead of burning or dumping plastic, their process uses chemistry and biology to recycle it on a molecular level, transforming trash into treasure.

It all started because two friends looked at a polluted river and refused to accept that it was hopeless.

Sometimes the biggest solutions begin with a question as simple as "why not?"

MORAL OF THE STORY

You don't have to wait to grow up to change the world. Every big discovery starts with someone young, curious, and brave enough to ask a new question. ●◆

The Shrimp with a Thunder Punch

Deep beneath the waves, in the warm waters of the Pacific Ocean, lives a tiny creature that looks harmless — like a small, colourful shrimp. But don't be fooled. This little fighter packs one of the most powerful punches in the entire animal kingdom.

Meet the mantis shrimp — a creature so quick, so strong, and so strange that scientists once thought their measurements had to be wrong.

There are more than 400 species of mantis shrimp, and they come in dazzling colours — emerald green, fiery red, electric blue. Some are small enough to fit on your fingertip; others grow as long as your forearm. But it's not their looks that make them famous — it's their punch.

At the end of each of their front legs are club-like limbs called raptorial appendages. When the shrimp hunts, it pulls those limbs back and snaps them forward faster than a speeding bullet.

Scientists measured the strike and discovered it moves at over 80 kilometres per hour — so fast that it creates a shockwave in the water. That shockwave can break glass aquarium walls, shatter shells, and even make a flash of light and heat as tiny bubbles collapse.

That's right — the mantis shrimp punches so hard it can boil water for an instant!

If you're a crab, snail, or clam, you don't stand a chance. One hit from a mantis shrimp can crack your shell open like a nut. Fishermen in tropical regions sometimes call it the "thumb splitter," because an accidental encounter can leave quite a mark.

But the shrimp doesn't just have power — it has supervision, too. Humans have three colour receptors in our eyes: red, green, and blue. The mantis shrimp has sixteen. It can see colours beyond our imagination — ultraviolet, polarised light, and patterns invisible to us. To the shrimp, the ocean must look like a rainbow explosion.

Scientists think this incredible vision helps them recognise each other's bright body patterns, spot prey in coral shadows, and even communicate using hidden colour signals.

For such a tiny creature, the mantis shrimp is a living mystery of nature's engineering. Its limbs are made of special bioceramic and protein layers, arranged like armour that doesn't crack under pressure.

Engineers have studied it to design stronger aeroplane materials and body armour.

Despite its fierce reputation, the mantis shrimp isn't evil or aggressive — it's simply built for survival. It hides in burrows, cleans itself carefully, and sometimes even pairs for life. When it's not hunting, it can be shy and curious, peeking out from coral like a tiny underwater boxer.

When you think of powerful animals, you might picture lions, sharks, or elephants. But this story proves that sometimes, the mightiest strength comes in the smallest package.

The mantis shrimp reminds us that nature's inventions aren't just big — they're brilliantly balanced, fine-tuned, and sometimes explosive.

MORAL OF THE STORY

Never underestimate small wonders. Power isn't always about size — sometimes it's about speed, precision, and perfect design. ✳🦐

The Octopus with a Coconut Shield

In the warm, shallow waters of Indonesia, an octopus glides silently across the sandy ocean floor. Its eight arms ripple like silk ribbons. Its eyes, bright and curious, scan the seabed for shells, stones, or — surprisingly — coconuts.

Meet the veined octopus, also called the coconut octopus, one of the cleverest creatures in the sea. While most octopuses use camouflage or ink to protect themselves, this little genius carries its own armour wherever it goes.

Scientists first discovered this behaviour by accident. In 2009, while studying coral reefs, divers noticed something unusual — an octopus dragging two hollow coconut shells across the sand. It struggled and stumbled, its tentacles wrapped awkwardly around the heavy halves. Then, to everyone's astonishment, it did something incredible.

The octopus placed one shell half on the ground, flipped its body inside, and pulled the second half over itself — like a knight lowering his helmet.

It wasn't just hiding; it was building a shelter.

This was the first time scientists had ever seen a sea animal use tools — something once thought only humans, apes, and a few birds could do. The octopus didn't just find protection; it planned. It carried its coconut armour for later use, a sign of intelligence that amazed researchers everywhere.

The veined octopus doesn't live in coral reefs or rocky caves like others do. It prefers the open seabed, where danger lurks — sharks, eels, and other predators cruise by. But with its trusty coconut halves, it's always prepared. When threatened, it scoops sand over itself, burrows down, and vanishes — only two watchful eyes peeking from beneath its shell.

This octopus is also a master of disguise. Its skin can change colour and texture in an instant. One moment, it looks like smooth coral; the next, it's rough and grainy like sand. It can mimic seaweed swaying in the current, or even flatten its body to slither like a flounder.

But the coconut trick remains its most astonishing act — proof of a mind that can imagine, plan, and problem-solve. Scientists believe this clever behaviour shows that octopuses are capable of complex thought, memory, creativity, and even a touch of curiosity.

Some divers have even seen the same octopus return to the same spot, retrieve the same coconuts, and rebuild its shelter after days away. It remembers.

And yet, despite its intelligence, the veined octopus lives a short life, only about a year or two. But in that time, it shows the world that brains don't have to come with bones.

The ocean is full of strange minds — and this one, hidden under a humble coconut, might just be one of the most remarkable of all.

MORAL OF THE STORY

Smart ideas can come from anyone — or anything. Sometimes the best protection isn't strength or speed, but imagination. ●🐙

The Explorer Who Mapped a Dream

Before satellites, before aeroplanes, before Google Maps — people explored the world by walking, sailing, and imagining.

They climbed mountains to see farther. They drew coastlines from memory. They traced rivers with ink and guessed what lay beyond. But one explorer saw more than just land and sea — he saw connections. He believed that understanding the Earth meant understanding ourselves.

His name was Alexander von Humboldt, and he didn't just travel the world — he felt it.

Born in 1769 in Berlin, Humboldt grew up surrounded by books, art, and science. As a boy, he collected rocks, bugs, and plants the way others collected toys. He was endlessly curious, not just about what things were, but how they fit together.

He once said, "The most dangerous worldview is the worldview of those who have not viewed the world."

When he grew up, he set out to do just that — to see the world.

In 1799, at the age of 29, Humboldt began his greatest journey — a five-year expedition through South America.

He and his friend Aimé Bonpland, a botanist from France, carried notebooks, barometers, thermometers, and measuring tools through dense jungles, rivers, and mountains.

They travelled along the Orinoco River, climbed the Andes Mountains, and even reached the edge of active volcanoes. Humboldt took notes on everything — air pressure, temperature, plants, animals, and even how people lived.

He wasn't looking for treasure or fame. He was mapping the patterns of life.

In Ecuador, he climbed the mighty Mount Chimborazo, which at the time was believed to be the tallest mountain in the world. Every step was agony, yet Humboldt stopped constantly — not to rest, but to record observations.

From that mountain, he had an idea that would change science forever. He noticed that the plants growing near the base were tropical — lush and green. Higher up, they became smaller and colder. And near the top, they vanished completely under the snow.

He realised that these climate zones repeated all over the planet — on mountains, across continents, and even under the sea. Everything on Earth was connected by invisible threads of temperature, elevation, and ecology.

He began to draw what he saw — a map of nature itself.

When he returned home, Humboldt's notebooks overflowed with data, sketches, and wonder. His famous diagram of Mount Chimborazo became one of the first ecological maps in history, showing how climate, geography, and biology work together.

His discoveries inspired Charles Darwin, who carried Humboldt's books on his own voyage aboard The Beagle. Darwin later said, "Humboldt kindled in me a burning zeal to add even the smallest contribution to natural science."

But perhaps Humboldt's greatest gift wasn't just his science — it was his vision of unity.

He wrote that the Earth was "a single great organism," and humans were part of it — not separate. He believed knowledge should connect, not divide.

When he died in 1859, he was called "the last man who knew everything." But really, he was the first to show that everything is connected.

He didn't just map the Earth. He mapped the dream of understanding it.

Moral of the Story

Exploration isn't just about finding new places — it's about seeing old places with new eyes. ●●

The Fish That Walks on Land

If you ever wander along a muddy mangrove swamp in Southeast Asia or Australia, you might see something that makes you blink twice. A fish — yes, a fish — clambering out of the water, squirming across the mud on its fins, blinking at you with eyes that stick out like periscopes.

That's no trick of the light. You've just met the mudskipper, one of the strangest — and cleverest — fish on Earth.

While most fish spend their whole lives underwater, the mudskipper spends half of its life on land. It can walk, climb, and even breathe air, making it a living link between the worlds of water and land — a reminder of what life might have looked like millions of years ago when creatures first crawled out of the sea.

The mudskipper's "legs" aren't real legs, of course — they're strong pectoral fins, which it uses like crutches. With a quick wiggle and push, it can hop across the mud in short bursts, almost like a frog.

Its skin is coated in a slimy layer that keeps it from drying out, and when the tide goes out, it takes full advantage of the exposed world above.

What does a fish do on land, you might wonder? Well, mudskippers are quite busy. They build burrows, hunt for insects and crabs, and even defend territories like tiny, slippery soldiers. Males dig deep tunnels into the mud and proudly guard them, popping out to chase away rivals with fin-flaring dances and dramatic leaps.

And those eyes! Mudskippers have bulging eyes on top of their heads, letting them see above and below the surface at once. When it rains, they blink — not with eyelids, but by pulling their eyes down into their heads to wash them clean. It's both gross and amazing!

Their homes, the mangrove swamps, are special too. Mangroves are trees that grow with their roots tangled in salty water, creating forests where fish and birds share space. Here, mudskippers play an important role — they dig burrows that help the mud breathe and let oxygen reach the roots of the trees.

Scientists are fascinated by these strange amphibious fish because they offer clues about evolution — how ancient sea creatures might have adapted to land long ago. Watching a mudskipper hop across a mangrove bank is like watching a chapter of Earth's story come to life.

Even with all their talents, mudskippers are vulnerable.

Pollution and habitat loss threaten their muddy homes.

But for now, as the tide rises and falls, they continue their daily dance between two worlds — swimming like fish, walking like frogs, and proving that life always finds creative ways to survive.

MORAL OF THE STORY

Adaptability is a superpower. When the world changes, the ones who thrive are those who learn to live between worlds. ●🐟

The Trees That Whisper Underground

Walk into a forest, and it might seem peaceful and quiet. You'll hear birds singing, leaves rustling, and the wind sighing through branches. But deep beneath your feet, something remarkable is happening — a secret conversation that no one can hear.

The forest is talking.

Under the soil, where roots twist and earthworms crawl, trees are connected by a vast invisible network made not of wires or internet cables, but of fungus. Yes — mushrooms!

Scientists call it the "mycorrhizal network," but some people call it the Wood Wide Web. It's a living underground web that connects trees to each other, allowing them to share food, send warnings, and even help their neighbours survive.

Here's how it works: The tiny threads of fungus — called hyphae — grow around and into tree roots, forming connections that let water and nutrients flow both ways.

The fungus helps the trees absorb minerals, and in return, the trees give the fungus sugar made from sunlight. It's a perfect friendship.

But that's just the beginning. Scientists discovered that these underground connections also act like communication lines. When a tree is attacked by insects or disease, it can send chemical signals through the network, warning nearby trees to prepare their defences.

Some trees even share food with others. For example, big, healthy trees — sometimes called "mother trees" — can send extra carbon to smaller or younger trees that are struggling in the shade. It's like a forest version of lending a helping hand.

Dr Suzanne Simard, a forest ecologist from Canada, was one of the first scientists to prove this. Using gentle experiments with labelled carbon dioxide, she showed how trees could pass nutrients through the soil — even between different species, like firs and birches.

Her research changed how people think about forests. Instead of trees competing for space and sunlight, she showed that they cooperate — living in communities that care for one another in complex, almost magical ways.

When one tree is cut down, its roots may still feed nearby seedlings for years. When a storm breaks a branch, neighbours seem to respond, sending more nutrients its way. The forest is alive with connection — quiet, ancient, and wise.

So the next time you walk in the woods, remember: even when it seems still, there's an entire world whispering beneath your feet.

Every root and mushroom strand tells the same story — that life is stronger when it's shared.

Moral of the Story

True strength grows through connection. Even the tallest trees need their friends to stand firm against the winds and weather. 🍄🖤

The Birds That Decorate Like Architects

Deep in the forests of Australia and New Guinea, there lives a bird with a hobby that would make any artist proud. While other birds spend their days searching for food or singing to attract mates, this one spends hours — even days — building something extraordinary: a work of art.

Meet the bowerbird, nature's most creative architect.

Male bowerbirds don't just build nests — they design bowers, special display structures built not for raising chicks, but for impressing females. Each bower is a personal art gallery, carefully crafted and decorated to show off the builder's taste, patience, and style.

There are many kinds of bowerbirds, and each has its own artistic flair. Some build tunnel-like halls of sticks. Others create open courts or even avenues lined with twigs and moss. Once the framework is done, the decorating begins.

That's when the fun starts.

Using their sharp eyes and beaks, bowerbirds collect colourful objects — berries, flowers, shells, stones, feathers, bottle caps, buttons, even bits of plastic humans leave behind. Each piece is chosen with care and arranged just so. Blue bowerbirds love blue things best, and will go to incredible lengths to find them — a scrap of blue ribbon, a shiny beetle shell, or even a lost pen cap.

When the bower is finished, it looks like something out of a fairy tale — a bird-sized art gallery glowing with colour. Then the male begins his performance. He sings, dances, and struts proudly, showing his bower to any nearby females, hoping one will be impressed enough to stay.

If she likes his taste and his moves, she might choose him as her mate. If not? She flies off to admire someone else's design — and the artist must start improving his masterpiece all over again.

What makes bowerbirds truly special isn't just their beauty — it's their intelligence. Scientists have studied them for years and discovered that these birds understand symmetry, colour contrast, and perspective. Some even arrange their decorations from large to small to create the illusion of a perfectly shaped bower — a trick called forced perspective, something humans use in art and photography!

The males constantly tweak their displays, replacing faded flowers and adjusting shiny objects to catch the light. In a way, they're doing interior design — bird style.

But the bower isn't a nest. Once mating is done, the female builds a separate nest elsewhere to raise her chicks. The bower is simply the male's stage, his love letter made of sticks and colour.

Each year, new generations of bowerbirds repeat the ritual, turning forest clearings into tiny art exhibitions. They remind us that beauty isn't just a human invention — it's a language written in feathers, song, and imagination.

Moral of the Story

Creativity isn't just for people. In nature, beauty can be a way of communicating — a sign of care, intelligence, and love. ♥🏠

The Frog That Freezes and Lives

Winter in the forests of North America can be fierce. The ponds freeze solid, the ground hardens like rock, and most small animals hide underground or hibernate deep in burrows. But one little creature doesn't hide at all — it freezes. Completely.

Meet the wood frog, the tiny amphibian that turns to ice and still lives to croak about it when spring returns.

Each autumn, as temperatures drop, most frogs hop into the mud below ponds to stay warm. But the wood frog does something entirely different. It stays on land, hides under leaves, and waits. When the first snowflakes fall, its body begins to change.

Its heart slows. Its breathing stops. Its blood freezes solid. Even its eyeballs turn to ice. In a matter of hours, the wood frog becomes a little frog-shaped popsicle — frozen stiff and silent.

You might think that means it's dead. But nature, as always, has a surprise.

Inside its body, the frog's liver releases a special kind of sugar called glucose, which works like antifreeze. It spreads through the frog's cells, protecting them from damage. The frog's organs stop working — but they don't break. They wait.

All winter long, while snow piles high and winds howl through the forest, hundreds of these frozen frogs lie hidden under layers of leaves and frost, motionless. Yet inside, they're quietly alive, suspended between life and death.

Then, when spring sunshine finally warms the forest, something magical happens.

The ice in their bodies melts. Their hearts begin to beat again. Their lungs start to breathe. Their skin softens. One by one, they twitch, move, and hop back into the world as if nothing happened at all. Within minutes, the forest is alive with choruses of croaking frogs, celebrating their thawed return.

Scientists have studied the wood frog's amazing survival trick to understand how its body endures such freezing. What they've learned could one day help humans preserve organs for transplants — or even make long-distance space travel possible.

Despite their small size, wood frogs are an important part of their ecosystem. They feed on insects, help control pest populations, and serve as food for birds and mammals.

Their yearly freeze-and-thaw cycle reminds us how creative nature can be when it comes to survival.

In the world of the wood frog, winter isn't an ending — it's just a long nap inside an icy blanket.

When you hear the first frog songs in spring, remember that each voice once lay silent and frozen, dreaming under the snow.

Moral of the Story

Sometimes survival means standing still. Patience, resilience, and a little science can thaw even the coldest challenges. ❄️🖤

The Desert That Blooms Overnight

Deserts are supposed to be empty — or so most people think. Hot, dry, and silent, with endless sand and rock stretching to the horizon. But once in a while, something astonishing happens.

In a single night, a desert can explode into colour.

It happens in places like the Atacama Desert in Chile, one of the driest places on Earth. Some parts of it can go years — even decades — without rain. The soil looks lifeless, cracked, and brown. The sun blazes by day, and the air freezes by night. It seems like nothing could ever grow there.

But hidden beneath that dusty surface is a secret: millions of tiny seeds, lying in wait.

These seeds can sleep for years, even decades, perfectly still. They wait for a sign — the soft touch of rain. And when it finally comes, even just a few drops, the desert awakens.

Within hours, roots burst from the seeds. Stems stretch upward. Petals unfurl. The entire landscape transforms into a sea of colour — purple, yellow, pink, and white flowers carpeting the sand as far as the eye can see.

This rare and magical event is called the "desierto florido," or "flowering desert."

It can happen only when rain falls at just the right time and in just the right amount. Too little, and the seeds stay asleep. Too much, and they drown. But when conditions are perfect, the desert becomes a garden overnight.

Scientists say it's one of the most extraordinary examples of adaptation on Earth.

These desert plants evolved to survive without rain for years, storing all their strength in tiny seeds that know when to wake up.

The flowering doesn't last long — just a few weeks. Then, as the heat returns and the soil dries, the flowers drop their seeds and fade away, leaving the desert bare again. But below the surface, the next generation waits patiently for the next miracle rain.

The Atacama isn't the only place where this happens. Similar bursts of life appear in the Mojave Desert in the United States, the Namib Desert in Africa, and even parts of Australia. Each time, it's a reminder that even in the harshest, driest places, life finds a way.

People who have seen it say it feels like standing in a dream — the air filled with the scent of flowers, bees buzzing, and butterflies drifting where only dust had been the day before.

The desert, it turns out, is never truly dead. It's just waiting — quietly storing its beauty until the right moment.

MORAL OF THE STORY

Patience and hope can bring beauty to even the driest places. Life doesn't disappear; it just waits for its chance to shine. 🌹🌵

The Mountain That Grows and Shrinks

Mountains are supposed to be strong and steady — the oldest, hardest parts of our planet. But one mountain in the middle of the world has a secret: it's always changing. Sometimes it grows, and sometimes it shrinks.

Meet Mount Everest, the tallest mountain on Earth. Rising high above the Himalayas on the border of Nepal and China, its summit stands so tall that climbers who reach the top can see the curve of the planet below them. Yet even this mighty peak isn't fixed in place.

Every year, Everest moves, grows taller by a few millimetres, and then — sometimes — drops back down again.

How is that possible?

To understand, we have to travel deep underground. Beneath the Earth's surface, giant pieces of rock called tectonic plates are always shifting, colliding, and sliding past one another. They move so slowly that we can't feel it — only a few centimetres a year — but over millions of years, their movement shapes entire continents.

Long ago, one of these plates — the Indian Plate — began drifting north and crashed into another, the Eurasian Plate. The collision was so powerful that it pushed up layers of rock to form the Himalayas, the world's highest mountain range. That process is still happening today. It's like the Earth is slowly crumpling up a giant rug.

That's why Mount Everest still grows taller by about 5 millimetres each year — the plates beneath it continue to collide, pushing it higher toward the sky.

But nature has a way of keeping balance. The same forces that lift Everest can also make it shrink.

When earthquakes shake the region, parts of the mountain's slopes can shift downward. In 2015, after a major earthquake in Nepal, scientists used satellites to measure Everest and discovered it had actually shrunk by about 2.5 centimetres!

Snow and wind shape it, too. Blizzards carve away rock, ice melts and refreezes, glaciers slide and scrape — constantly reshaping the mountain's crown. Even though it looks eternal, Everest is alive with movement.

Climbers who reach the top often describe standing on a mountain that feels timeless — yet they're really standing on a moment in Earth's long story, a story still being written.

Mount Everest isn't alone in this. Other mountains around the world — from the Andes in South America to the Rockies in North America — also rise and fall with the slow dance of tectonic plates. But Everest is special because it reminds us that even the highest, hardest places on Earth are still part of a living, changing planet.

And that's what makes our world so extraordinary.

The mountains breathe. The Earth grows. And everything — even stone — is always becoming something new.

MORAL OF THE STORY

Even giants change with time. Strength isn't about staying still — it's about growing, shifting, and adapting with the world around you. ▲●

The Student Who Measured the Invisible

The world is full of things we can't see. Air. Sound. Magnetism. Even the pull of gravity — invisible hands shaping everything around us.

But for most of history, people could only guess at what was hidden beyond their sight. Then, one determined student found a way to measure the invisible.

His name was Michael Faraday, and he grew up in London in the early 1800s — a time when electricity was still a mystery and magic seemed to flow through copper wires.

Michael's family was poor. He had little schooling and started work at just thirteen, delivering newspapers and binding books. But while most boys hurried through their chores, Michael read the books he was meant to deliver. He devoured every page about science and discovery, fascinated by experiments with light, air, and energy.

He couldn't afford a formal education, but that didn't stop him from learning.

One day, a kind customer gave him tickets to a public lecture by Sir Humphry Davy, one of the most famous scientists of the time. Davy's lectures at the Royal Institution were dazzling — explosions, glowing gases, and electric sparks. To young Michael, it was like watching lightning being tamed.

Afterwards, he gathered his courage and sent Davy a letter — carefully written, bound in leather, filled with notes and sketches he'd made. He asked for a chance to work in Davy's lab.

To his surprise, Davy said yes.

Faraday became his assistant, cleaning bottles, preparing chemicals, and writing notes. It wasn't glamorous work, but it was everything he'd dreamed of. Slowly, he began to design his own experiments.

Michael didn't just want to make electricity. He wanted to understand it. What was it? Why did it move? Could it be related to magnetism — another invisible force?

He began to play with magnets, wires, and coils of metal, searching for connections. For years, he saw nothing unusual. But one day in 1831, as he passed a magnet near a coil of wire, a needle on his measuring device twitched.

The invisible had moved something visible. He had discovered electromagnetic induction — the principle that moving a magnet near a wire can create an electric current.

That single discovery changed the world. It became the foundation of electric generators and transformers, the very machines that power every city, home, and lightbulb today.

Faraday had measured the invisible — the unseen dance between magnetism and electricity that powers the modern world.

But what made Michael truly special wasn't just his discovery — it was his humility. He remained gentle and kind all his life, often saying, "Nothing is too wonderful to be true."

He believed that science wasn't about showing off what you know — it was about uncovering what everyone can understand. Even Queen Victoria attended his lectures, where he explained invisible forces using everyday objects like soap bubbles, candles, and spinning coils.

Michael Faraday proved that greatness doesn't come from privilege — it comes from curiosity, patience, and wonder.

He never went to college. He never became rich. But he built the foundation of modern physics — all because he dared to measure what no one could see.

MORAL OF THE STORY

You don't need to see something to believe in it. Curiosity and imagination can make the invisible visible. ⚡🔍

The River That Disappears Underground

Rivers usually flow proudly across the land — twisting and turning through forests, cities, and valleys before finally meeting the sea. But somewhere in the world, there are rivers that seem to vanish. They run strong and sparkling one moment, and then — suddenly — they're gone.

One of the most mysterious of them all is the Puerto Princesa Underground River in the Philippines, a hidden wonder that flows not across the earth, but beneath it.

This strange river begins high in the mountain forests of Palawan Island, winding its way through thick jungle and limestone cliffs. Then, as it nears the coast, it does something magical — it dives underground, slipping into a dark cave and continuing its journey through the heart of the mountain.

For almost eight kilometres, the river travels through twisting tunnels and vast chambers before finally emerging into the sea on the other side. It's as if the Earth itself swallowed it whole and then gently released it again.

Inside, the cave is breathtaking. The walls glitter with stalactites and stalagmites — stone formations shaped over thousands of years by dripping water. The air is cool and echoes with the sound of dripping, rushing, and the flutter of wings. Colonies of bats and swallows live high above the river, their calls bouncing off the cave ceiling.

Tourists who visit today ride small boats with headlamps, floating silently through the darkness while guides point out shapes in the rocks — a dragon, a cathedral, even a face that seems to smile down from the stone. The water glows a soft turquoise under the lamplight, like liquid glass.

Scientists believe the underground river was formed millions of years ago, when rainwater mixed with carbon dioxide from the air to create a weak acid. Over time, that water slowly dissolved the limestone rock, carving out tunnels big enough for an entire river to flow through.

And it's not the only one of its kind. All over the world — in Mexico, Slovenia, New Zealand, and Vietnam — hidden rivers flow through underground mazes of stone. But the Puerto Princesa River is special because it's one of the longest navigable underground rivers on Earth, and it connects directly to the sea.

In 2011, it was named one of the New Seven Wonders of Nature, alongside the Amazon and the Great Barrier Reef. But for the people who live nearby, it's always been more than just a wonder — it's a reminder that the planet still holds mysteries we're only beginning to understand.

From above, the jungle hums with life. From below, the river whispers its ancient secrets, echoing through stone halls that no sunlight ever touches.

It's a place where Earth's heart still beats — quietly, beautifully, and unseen.

MORAL OF THE STORY

Not everything that disappears is gone. Some of the world's greatest wonders flow quietly beneath the surface. ●💧

The Lake That Disappears and Returns

Most lakes are calm, reliable mirrors of water — places where fish swim, birds glide, and mountains reflect their faces. But there's one lake on Earth that refuses to stay put.

Every year, it vanishes. And then, just as suddenly, it comes back.

This strange and beautiful place is called Lake Cerknica, hidden among the green hills of Slovenia in Europe. To people who live nearby, it's known as Cerkniško jezero — "the lake that comes and goes."

If you visit it in the spring, you'll see a sparkling blue lake stretching for miles, dotted with ducks, frogs, and tall reeds. Fishermen paddle quietly across its surface, and children skip stones along its banks. It looks like any other peaceful lake — until summer arrives.

Then something amazing happens.

The water begins to sink. Day by day, it lowers, revealing muddy meadows, then grassy fields, and finally dry land.

Within weeks, the lake vanishes completely, leaving behind nothing but a green valley filled with wildflowers, grazing cows, and farmers walking where fish once swam.

To the untrained eye, it seems like magic. But there's real science behind it.

Beneath Lake Cerknica lies a vast underground maze of caves, tunnels, and sinkholes, carved out of limestone rock over millions of years. The region is part of what geologists call karst landscape — the same type of terrain that creates underground rivers and hidden caves around the world.

During wet seasons, when heavy rains and melting snow fill the valley, the water rushes down from the surrounding hills. The underground channels become full, and the lake rises, spreading wide and deep across the plain.

But as the dry season comes and the rains fade, the opposite happens. The water drains away through sinkholes — natural holes in the ground that act like hidden drains. Slowly, the lake slips back underground, returning to the caverns below until the next big rainfall.

The cycle repeats every year: appearance, disappearance, return. To the people of Slovenia, it's a rhythm as old as time.

In the 17th century, even the great scientist Johann Weikhard von Valvasor studied this disappearing lake.

His detailed observations and drawings of Lake Cerknica's strange behaviour were so remarkable that he was invited to join the Royal Society of London — one of the world's oldest scientific organisations. His work helped introduce Europe to the mysterious beauty of karst landscapes.

Today, Lake Cerknica is a protected nature park and a paradise for wildlife. When it's full, it becomes the largest lake in Slovenia, home to over 270 species of birds, including herons, ducks, and rare storks. When it dries, it transforms into meadows filled with butterflies, frogs, and blooming flowers.

It's like having two worlds in one — a water world and a grassland world — taking turns throughout the year.

Locals have learned to live with the lake's rhythm. Some build floating houses that rise and fall with the water. Others plant crops in the fertile soil once the lake drains away.

Lake Cerknica reminds us that not all disappearances are losses. Sometimes, they're just part of nature's breathing — an inhale, an exhale, a promise to return.

MORAL OF THE STORY

Change isn't an ending — it's part of nature's rhythm. What disappears today might return tomorrow, stronger and more beautiful than before. 💧🌿

The Ice That Burns Blue

Ice and fire — two opposites that can't exist together. Ice freezes; fire burns. One melts, the other destroys. But what if there were a kind of ice that could burn?

Deep in the cold seafloors and frozen tundras of the world, scientists have found something that seems impossible — a mysterious, glowing "fire ice" that looks like ordinary snow but can catch flame when lit.

It's called methane hydrate, or more poetically, "burning ice."

At first glance, it seems like magic. Imagine picking up a chunk of white, frozen crystal, only to see a blue flame dancing on its surface without melting it. It crackles and flickers just like a candle, even though your hands feel cold. But the secret isn't magic — it's science.

Methane hydrate forms when two things meet under the right conditions: freezing temperatures and high pressure.

Far below the ocean floor, where sunlight never reaches, tiny bubbles of methane gas — produced by ancient plants and sea creatures trapped in the mud — get surrounded by water molecules. The water freezes around the gas in cage-like crystals, locking the methane inside. The result is a frozen mixture that looks like ice but contains enormous energy.

If that ice is brought to the surface and warmed, the methane escapes as gas, and when you light it, it burns with a bright blue flame. Hence the name: ice that burns.

Scientists first discovered methane hydrate in the 1960s, but it wasn't until later that they realised just how much of it exists. These icy deposits are hidden all around the world — under the Arctic permafrost, along the coasts of Japan and India, beneath the Gulf of Mexico, and even off the shores of Alaska. Some experts estimate that the total energy trapped in methane hydrate could be twice as much as all the coal, oil, and natural gas on Earth combined!

That sounds like a treasure — but it's also a warning.

Methane is a powerful greenhouse gas, even stronger than carbon dioxide. If the planet's temperatures rise and large amounts of methane hydrate melt, that gas could escape into the atmosphere, speeding up global warming. It's a sleeping giant beneath our feet — both a promise and a danger.

To learn more, scientists have begun carefully studying methane hydrate deposits in frozen places like Siberia, Canada, and Antarctica. In 2013, Japan became the first country to successfully extract methane hydrate from the seafloor and use it as fuel. But it's tricky — disturb the balance too much, and the fragile ice structures can collapse or release gas too quickly.

Still, this strange "burning ice" fascinates researchers. It's a reminder that the world holds hidden forms of energy, waiting in silence under oceans and ice caps. Nature's inventions often defy what we think we know — fire trapped in ice, light glowing in darkness, warmth hiding inside the coldest places.

And maybe, one day, this discovery will help humanity move toward cleaner energy — if we can learn to unlock it wisely.

For now, methane hydrate sleeps quietly in its frozen homes, blue fire waiting within the white.

It's proof that even opposites — fire and ice — can share the same space, if nature wills it.

MORAL OF THE STORY

The world is full of paradoxes — moments where opposites unite. True wonder lives where fire meets ice, and knowledge meets respect. 🔥❄️

The Island That Vanished in a Day

Islands usually take thousands of years to form. Volcanoes erupt, coral grows, or rivers drop enough sand to build new land. But there's one island in the world that appeared suddenly, almost overnight — and then disappeared just as fast.

This is the story of Hunga Tonga-Hunga Ha'apai, the island that was born from fire, lived for a few short years, and vanished in a single, thunderous day.

The story begins deep beneath the South Pacific Ocean, near the small island nation of Tonga. Beneath the waves lies a ring of volcanoes, part of the fiery "Pacific Ring of Fire," where the Earth's crust is restless and alive.

In December 2014, sailors and local villagers noticed something strange on the horizon — clouds of grey smoke rising from the sea. The ocean bubbled and hissed as black ash burst into the air. The smell of sulfur drifted for miles. What they were witnessing was a volcanic eruption, but not from land — it was coming from the seafloor.

For days, explosions sent plumes of ash, gas, and steam thousands of meters into the sky. When the eruption finally slowed, the world watched in amazement as something new emerged: a mound of dark volcanic rock rising above the waves.

An island had been born.

It was small at first — just a few hundred meters across — but within weeks, it grew large enough to walk on. Scientists from Tonga and NASA flew over it, snapping pictures of what looked like a black scar on the blue ocean. They named it Hunga Tonga–Hunga Ha'apai, after the two older islands it formed between.

The new land was made of volcanic ash and rock, fragile but fascinating. Over time, wind and rain began to shape it. Seabirds landed and built nests. Seeds carried by the wind began to sprout. Slowly, life began to take root.

Scientists were thrilled. It was the first new island of its kind to form and survive long enough to be studied by satellites. They thought it might last decades — maybe even centuries — giving clues about how volcanic islands like Hawaii and Iceland once began.

But the Earth had other plans.

In January 2022, almost eight years after its birth, the volcano beneath Hunga Tonga–Hunga Ha'apai awoke again.

At first, the eruptions were small.

Then, on January 15, 2022, came one of the most powerful explosions in modern history. The blast was so strong that it was heard more than 10,000 kilometres away — even as far as Alaska. Satellites captured a huge mushroom cloud of ash rising 58 kilometres into the sky, higher than any aeroplane could fly.

When the dust finally cleared, the island was gone.

The mighty explosion had blown away nearly all of Hunga Tonga-Hunga Ha'apai, leaving only a few jagged edges of rock where it once stood. The ocean had reclaimed what fire had created.

In the end, the island's short life — less than a decade — taught scientists more about Earth's raw power than any textbook could. It showed how quickly the planet can build and destroy, reminding us that our world is always changing, always alive.

MORAL OF THE STORY

Even the strongest things can be fleeting. Change is not destruction — it's Earth's way of starting over. 🌋

The Mistake That Saved Humanity

Some of the greatest discoveries in history didn't come from perfect plans or genius moments — they came from mistakes. But what separates a failure from a discovery is one small thing: curiosity.

That's exactly what happened to Alexander Fleming, the man who accidentally changed medicine — and saved millions of lives — because he refused to ignore what looked like a failure.

It all began in London, 1928, inside a quiet laboratory at St. Mary's Hospital. Fleming was a Scottish scientist studying bacteria — tiny invisible organisms that caused infections like pneumonia, strep throat, and gangrene. He spent his days growing colonies of bacteria in glass dishes filled with jelly-like nutrient gel, carefully labelling each one.

Then one summer, Fleming went on vacation and left his messy lab behind. Dishes covered the tables, some stacked, others forgotten on windowsills. When he returned, he started sorting through them — and that's when he noticed something strange.

On one plate, where bacteria had been growing thickly, there was a clear circle — a patch where no bacteria survived.

At the centre of that circle was a fuzzy blue-green mould.
Instead of throwing it away, Fleming leaned in closer. Most scientists might have said, "Oops, contamination!" and tossed it in the bin. But Fleming didn't see a mistake — he saw a mystery.

He wondered, What if this mould isn't ruining my experiment... what if it's doing something important?

So he began testing it.

He scraped some of the mould into a new dish and found that it stopped bacteria from growing there too. He repeated the test again and again, each time with the same result. The mould wasn't an accident — it was a natural bacteria killer.

Fleming had discovered penicillin, the world's first antibiotic.

It took years of teamwork with other scientists to turn that discovery into a usable medicine, but eventually, penicillin became the drug that changed everything.

During World War II, it saved the lives of millions of soldiers and civilians who would have died from infections that today seem minor — a small cut, a cough, a scratch.

Before penicillin, even a paper cut could turn deadly. After it, humanity had a weapon against disease.

Fleming's discovery wasn't neat, perfect, or planned. It came from a mistake, from curiosity, and from his belief that science is about noticing what others overlook.

He later joked, "One sometimes finds what one is not looking for." But what he really meant was this: you only find new things if you're willing to look at the unexpected — and ask why.

Fleming became one of the most famous scientists in history, winning the Nobel Prize in 1945. But if you'd asked him, he'd probably have said that all he did was keep his eyes open.

Because science isn't about avoiding mistakes — it's about learning from them.

MORAL OF THE STORY

Mistakes don't end discoveries — they begin them. The real secret of genius is curiosity, not perfection. 💡🌿

The Inventor Who Talked to Lightning

Some people see a thunderstorm and run for cover. Others count the seconds between flash and thunder. But one man — Nikola Tesla — looked at lightning and saw a conversation waiting to happen.

He wanted to understand it. He wanted to speak its language.

Born in 1856 in a small village in what is now Croatia, Tesla was a curious child who loved light, sound, and energy. His mother, though not formally educated, invented household tools from scraps, and his father was a storyteller. Between invention and imagination, Nikola's mind was already sparking.

As a boy, he was fascinated by the crackle of static electricity — the kind that makes your hair stand up when you touch metal after walking on a carpet. "There is power here," he told his mother. "Power that can move the world."

He wasn't wrong.

Years later, Tesla grew into a tall, quiet man with bright eyes and ideas far ahead of his time. He moved to New York City in the late 1800s, a period when the world was just learning to harness electricity. Streets were still lit by gas lamps, and most people had never seen a lightbulb.

Tesla believed electricity could be used for everything — light, communication, and energy for all people.

Working briefly for another inventor, Thomas Edison, Tesla soon realised they didn't share the same dream. Edison wanted practical inventions that made money; Tesla wanted to discover how nature itself worked — how energy flowed invisibly through the world.

So Tesla struck out on his own.

He created the alternating current (AC) system — a way of sending electricity long distances safely and efficiently. His design powered entire cities and became the foundation of the modern electric grid we use today.

But that wasn't enough. Tesla wanted to go further — to understand the very language of lightning.

In 1899, he built a laboratory in colourado Springs, a place famous for its wide-open skies and powerful storms. There, he experimented with massive coils — tall copper spirals that produced bolts of electricity several meters long.

When the machines roared to life, the entire lab flickered with blue light. Thunder rumbled through the ground. Sparks leapt between metal rods like living snakes of fire. Townspeople said they could see lightning dancing above Tesla's roof from miles away.

Tesla called it his "talk with the lightning."

He believed energy from storms could be captured and used to power the world — electricity sent wirelessly through the air, the same way sound travelled through radio waves. It was an idea no one else dared to dream of.

One night, while testing his equipment, Tesla's instruments picked up strange rhythmic signals. He wondered if they were from outer space — perhaps even messages from another planet. Scientists today think they were likely from lightning bouncing around the atmosphere, but to Tesla, they were proof that the universe itself was speaking.

Though many of his grandest ideas were too advanced for his time, Tesla's experiments laid the foundation for wireless communication, radio, and modern electrical systems.

MORAL OF THE STORY

Curiosity doesn't just follow the light — it creates it. When you listen closely enough, even lightning will answer back. ⚡🔔

WATER

The Teacher Who Lit Up the Dark

Some people change the world by discovering something new. Others change it by sharing what's already there — by turning sparks of knowledge into flames of hope.

That's what Anne Sullivan, a young teacher with unshakable patience, did for a girl who lived in silence and darkness.

Her student's name was Helen Keller.

Helen was born in 1880 in Alabama, USA. When she was just a baby, she became very sick — so sick that she lost both her sight and hearing before she was two years old.

To Helen, the world was a place of endless shadows and silence. She couldn't see her parents' faces or hear their voices. She could feel sunlight, rain, and vibrations of footsteps, but she couldn't understand words.

By the time she was six, Helen was wild with frustration. She screamed, kicked, and broke things. No one could reach her — until Anne Sullivan arrived.

Anne knew what it was like to live in darkness. She had grown up poor and nearly blind herself, living in an orphanage. But through her own struggle, she had learned something powerful: education was a kind of light.

When she met Helen, Anne was only twenty years old — barely out of school herself. Yet she came with more courage than most people twice her age.

On her very first day in the Keller home, Helen threw tantrums and refused to listen. But Anne didn't yell. She took Helen's hand gently and began to spell words into her palm using sign language.

She pressed the letters for D-O-L-L into Helen's small hand while letting her touch a real doll. Helen didn't understand at first. To her, the letters were just meaningless movements.

So Anne kept going — patiently, quietly, day after day.

Then came the breakthrough.

One afternoon, Anne led Helen outside to a water pump. She placed one of Helen's hands under the cool flow of water and spelt W-A-T-E-R into the other.

Suddenly, Helen froze. She tilted her head as if listening with her whole body.

She touched the water again, then Anne's hand — and spelt the word back.

Water," her fingers said.

In that moment, a door in Helen's mind opened. The world flooded in. She understood that everything had a name — and that words were keys.

From that day forward, Helen couldn't learn fast enough.

She wanted to know the names of everything — earth, tree, mother, love. Anne taught her tirelessly, spelling out every sound, every idea, every dream.

Years later, Helen would go on to graduate from college, write books, travel the world, and inspire millions. But she always said that without Anne, she would have remained in darkness.

And Anne? She never stopped teaching. Her patience became legendary. She once said, "My heart is singing for joy this morning. A miracle has happened! The light of understanding has shone upon my little pupil's mind."

The light she spoke of wasn't from a lamp or a sunrise — it was from learning.

MORAL OF THE STORY

Knowledge is light — and teachers are the ones who carry the torch. Even the smallest spark can brighten the darkest world.

The Girl Who Drew the First Dinosaur

Long before museums displayed towering skeletons and children could name dinosaurs like Tyrannosaurus rex or Triceratops, the very idea of "giant extinct reptiles" was unbelievable.

But one curious woman helped the world see them for the first time — not by digging them up, but by drawing them into existence.

Her name was Mary Ann Mantell.

In 1822, she was walking along a quiet country road in Sussex, England, while her husband, Dr. Gideon Mantell, stopped to visit one of his patients. The day was warm, and the gravel path glittered with bits of stone.

As she waited, Mary Ann bent down and picked up something odd — a chunk of rock with a strange tooth embedded in it. It wasn't flat or smooth like a normal fossil. It was sharp, curved, and ridged — like the tooth of some enormous plant-eating creature.

When her husband returned, she showed it to him. Gideon, a doctor and amateur fossil collector, was amazed.

He had seen many fossils before — shells, fish, and bones from ancient seas — but never anything like this.

He studied the tooth and compared it to modern animals. It didn't match any he knew. Finally, he realised it resembled the tooth of an iguana — but much, much larger.

They called it the Iguanodon, meaning "iguana tooth."

But at the time, no one believed them. Scientists scoffed. They said the Mantells were mistaken — that the fossil was probably from a fish or a rhinoceros. The idea that a giant reptile could have once roamed England was absurd.

Mary Ann didn't argue. She drew.

Using her skill as an illustrator, she created detailed sketches of the fossils her husband found — teeth, bones, and footprints. Her drawings were so careful and lifelike that scientists couldn't ignore them. Through her art, she gave shape to something no one had ever seen.

She made the invisible visible.

Eventually, the Mantells uncovered more fossils: pieces of limbs, vertebrae, and claws. Mary Ann drew each one, connecting them like a puzzle. Bit by bit, a new creature began to emerge — an enormous lizard-like animal that ate plants and walked on four legs.

It was the first creature ever identified as a dinosaur, though the word "dinosaur" (meaning "terrible lizard") wouldn't be coined until years later.

Her drawings were published in her husband's books and journals, spreading wonder across Europe. Children and scholars alike marvelled at the thought of these prehistoric giants.

But history often forgets quiet hands. For many years, Mary Ann's contribution was overshadowed by her husband's name, even though her discovery of that first fossil — and her drawings — helped science imagine a world long gone.

Today, we know that she was one of the first people to uncover and record evidence of a creature millions of years old — a true pioneer of palaeontology.

Mary Ann Mantell never called herself a scientist. But her curiosity, patience, and artistic eye changed how humans picture the past. She showed that discovery isn't only about finding — it's also about seeing.

MORAL OF THE STORY

You don't need a shovel to make a discovery. Sometimes, the most powerful tools are your eyes, your hands, and your imagination.

The Fossil Hunter on the Stormy Beach

More than two hundred years ago, in a small seaside town called Lyme Regis in England, the cliffs were alive with secrets — ancient bones, buried shells, and the stony remains of creatures that hadn't walked the Earth in millions of years.

And the person who discovered many of those secrets wasn't a famous scientist or an explorer with fancy tools. It was a young girl named Mary Anning.

Mary was born in 1799. Her family was poor, and life by the sea wasn't easy. Their tiny house stood near the bottom of a steep, crumbling cliff. When storms hit, rocks tumbled down, revealing strange shapes hidden inside the stone — twisted shells, spiny fish, and giant bones.

Mary's father, Richard Anning, made extra money by collecting and selling these "curiosities" to travellers. He taught Mary how to spot fossils buried in the cliffs — how to look for the faint outline of a bone or shell beneath layers of rock. She learned fast.

By the time she was ten, she could climb cliffs barefoot, hammer in hand, and carefully chip away at stone to reveal treasures from long ago.

But when Mary was only eleven, tragedy struck. Her father died suddenly, leaving her family with very little money. To survive, Mary kept fossil hunting. She sold the ones she found to visitors who came to the seaside — but she also dreamed of making a big discovery, one that would change how people saw the world.

One stormy winter's morning, the waves had ripped away part of the cliff. When the sky cleared, Mary went out searching. She spotted something enormous sticking out of the rock — something that looked like a skull, with teeth as big as her fingers!

Over many months, she carefully uncovered the full skeleton. It turned out to be nearly 17 feet long, with paddle-like limbs and a long, curved jaw. People had never seen anything like it. Some thought it was a crocodile. Others whispered it was a dragon.

But Mary had found something far older and stranger. Scientists later realised it was the first complete skeleton of an ichthyosaur, an ancient sea reptile that lived during the time of the dinosaurs.

Her discovery changed history. It helped prove that giant creatures had once ruled the seas — and that the world had existed for far longer than people had imagined.

Over the years, Mary made many more discoveries, including the first complete plesiosaur and the first British pterosaur (a flying reptile). Though she never went to university, scientists from across Europe came to see her work. They studied her fossils, learned from her notes, and even bought specimens for museums.

Still, many didn't give her credit. In those days, women weren't often recognised for scientific discoveries. But Mary never gave up. She kept exploring, climbing, and uncovering the mysteries of Earth's deep past.

Today, she is remembered as the Mother of Palaeontology — the girl from the stormy beach who brought the ancient world to light.

MORAL OF THE STORY

Even if the world overlooks you, your discoveries can still change it. Curiosity and persistence can dig up the past — and shape the future.

The Man Who Counted the Stars Twice

Every night, the sky glows with billions of stars — so many that it seems impossible to count them. Most of us look up, admire them, and move on. But one man decided not just to look — he decided to listen to the stars through light.

His name was William Herschel, and he saw the universe differently.

In the 1700s, William wasn't a scientist. He was a musician. Born in Germany, he played the oboe and conducted orchestras in England. But when he wasn't rehearsing, he spent his nights peering through tiny telescopes, trying to understand the heavens.

The stars fascinated him like musical notes — each shining at its own pitch and rhythm. "The sky," he said, "is full of harmony."

William wanted to see deeper into that harmony than anyone ever had. But the small telescopes of his time couldn't see far enough. So he built his own — grinding and polishing mirrors by hand in his backyard.

His sister, Caroline Herschel, worked beside him. Night after night, she mixed chemicals, cleaned glass, and recorded his observations. Together, they became a team — one measuring the sky, the other organising the universe.

One night in 1781, William noticed a tiny, fuzzy point of light moving differently from the stars around it. He watched it carefully. A few nights later, he checked again — it had shifted.

He had discovered something no one had ever seen before: a new planet.

He named it Uranus — the first planet found since ancient times, and the first discovered with a telescope. It was proof that the solar system was bigger than anyone had imagined.

The discovery changed astronomy forever. But William didn't stop there. He wanted to understand how the stars themselves were arranged.

So, he did something extraordinary: he decided to count them.

Using his massive handmade telescope — one of the largest in the world — William divided the sky into sections. Caroline would call out coordinates, and William would count every star visible in each part. Then they'd record the numbers and move to the next patch of sky.

They did this hundreds of times, night after night, in cold and heat, through fog and exhaustion.

When they finished, they had counted more than 90,000 stars.

From that data, William drew one of the first maps of the Milky Way — a glowing spiral of stars with our Sun nestled among them.

He had measured the shape of the galaxy by counting points of light — twice, to be sure it wasn't a mistake.

But his curiosity didn't end there. In 1800, while experimenting with sunlight and prisms, William discovered infrared radiation — a kind of invisible light beyond the colours we can see. Once again, he revealed something that had always been there but unseen.

MORAL OF THE STORY

The universe rewards those who look twice — once with their eyes, and once with their heart. ✨🔭

The Boy Who Chased the Northern Lights

On cold winter nights in Norway, when the snow lay heavy on the rooftops and the stars shimmered like ice, people would whisper about the aurora — ribbons of green and pink light that danced across the sky.

They called it the northern lights, a miracle, a mystery, even a spirit. Some said it was the reflection of fish swimming under the frozen sea. Others believed it was the souls of ancestors playing among the stars.

But one boy, named Kristian Birkeland, wanted to know the truth.

He didn't want to explain the lights with myths. He wanted to follow them — to chase them through snow and silence until he understood their language.

Kristian was born in 1867 in Christiania (now Oslo), Norway. He loved science, magnets, and storms — anything that glowed or sparked. As a child, he would rub amber against wool to make static crackle in the dark and wonder if the same invisible force powered the aurora.

When he grew up, he became a physicist — a scientist who studies energy and forces. But even as an adult, he still stared out his window at night, watching the sky come alive with colour.

What made the heavens dance? What made green fire flow like rivers above the world?

To find out, Kristian built machines.

In a small laboratory, he set up a magnetised metal sphere to represent Earth and surrounded it with electric currents. He darkened the room and turned on the power. Instantly, streaks of purple and green light began to glow around the poles of the sphere — tiny auroras!

He called his invention the terrella, or "little Earth." With it, he showed that the northern lights were caused by electrically charged particles from the Sun striking Earth's magnetic field — creating glowing arcs high in the atmosphere.

He had captured the sky in a box.

But Kristian didn't stop there. He wanted proof — real, shimmering proof. So he led expeditions into Norway's frozen north, where the auroras blazed brightest.

He and his team hauled heavy scientific instruments through snow and wind, setting up magnetic detectors in lonely cabins far above the Arctic Circle.

Many nights, he stood outside for hours, frost forming in his beard, eyes fixed on the swirling lights.

When others saw beauty, he saw data. When others saw mystery, he saw messages — nature's signals written in colour.

Through his work, Kristian became the first scientist to explain the true cause of the northern lights. He revealed that our planet and the Sun are connected by invisible lines of magnetism — a cosmic dance of energy between worlds.

He proved that the aurora wasn't just a miracle of the sky, but a story of physics — the Sun whispering to the Earth in light.

Today, satellites and observatories confirm what Kristian discovered more than a century ago. And yet, his work still feels like magic — the perfect mix of science and wonder.

Kristian Birkeland didn't just chase the northern lights. He caught them — and taught the world that even the coldest skies are alive with fire.

MORAL OF THE STORY

The universe speaks in colour, and curiosity is how we learn to read it. ■✦

The Explorer Who Found a Mountain Under the Sea

Most explorers look up — to mountains, skies, and stars. But one woman looked down, into the deepest blue of all.

Her name was Marie Tharp, and she made one of the most important maps in human history — without ever leaving her desk.

Marie was born in 1920 in Michigan, USA. Her father was a mapmaker for the U.S. government, and from the time she could walk, she followed him across fields and rivers, collecting soil samples and watching him draw lines that shaped the world.

But Marie didn't just want to draw what people could see — she wanted to draw what they couldn't.

When she grew up, she studied geology — the science of Earth's structure — but it wasn't easy. In those days, few women were allowed in the field. Many professors told her that geology was "a man's subject."

Still, Marie didn't stop. She earned her degree and found a job at Columbia University, helping scientists who studied the oceans.

At that time, the ocean floor was mostly a mystery. People thought it was flat and featureless — a dark, empty desert beneath the waves. No one had ever truly mapped it, because no human could dive that deep.

But Marie realised there was another way.

Her colleague Bruce Heezen led research ships that used echo sounding — a technique that sent sound waves down through the water and measured how long they took to bounce back. The data came back as endless columns of numbers.

To most people, those numbers were meaningless. To Marie, they were clues.

She spread the long sheets of data across her desk — miles of numbers stretching like a secret code — and began to plot each depth point by hand on enormous sheets of paper. Slowly, a pattern began to emerge.

The ocean floor wasn't flat at all.

It had ridges, valleys, and cliffs — underwater mountains as tall as the Himalayas.

Then, in the middle of the Atlantic Ocean, she noticed something astonishing: a deep, narrow valley running straight down the centre of a mountain range. It looked exactly like the rift valleys she'd studied on land — the kind formed when continents move apart.

Marie realised what she was seeing: proof of plate tectonics — the idea that Earth's continents drift and reshape the planet over time.

It was one of the greatest discoveries in geology.

But when she showed her maps to her male colleagues, they laughed. "It's just girl talk," one said. "The ocean floor doesn't have mountains."

Marie stayed calm. She kept mapping. She let the data — not her words — do the talking.

When the next research ship returned with new sonar readings, the results matched her drawings exactly. The underwater mountain range was real. The central valley was real.

Marie Tharp had discovered the Mid-Atlantic Ridge, an enormous chain of volcanoes stretching across the ocean floor — proof that the Earth's crust was alive and moving.

Her maps transformed our understanding of the planet. They showed that the seafloor wasn't a still, silent world, but a place of creation — where new land was born beneath the waves.

Moral of the Story

You don't always have to go far to make a discovery. Sometimes, you just have to look deeper — and believe what the data tells you.

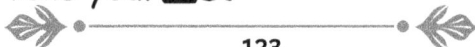

The Student Who Heard a New Star

On a quiet evening in 1967, a young woman sat alone in a radio lab at the University of Cambridge. Her name was Jocelyn Bell, and she was a graduate student studying astronomy — one of the few women in her field at the time.

While most people looked at stars through telescopes, Jocelyn was listening to them. Her team had built a strange-looking machine made of wires, poles, and antennas stretched across a field. It didn't take pictures of stars; it recorded radio waves — invisible signals coming from space.

Every day, Jocelyn sat at her desk, flipping through endless rolls of paper charts printed from the machine. The lines zigzagged across the pages like heartbeats. Most of them showed static — noisy blips made by lightning, planes, or even passing cars. But Jocelyn was patient. She checked every line carefully, just in case something special hid inside the noise.

Then one day, she saw it.

Amid the usual messy squiggles, there appeared a tiny, regular pulse. It wasn't random like lightning or static. It was neat, repeating every 1.3 seconds — tick, tick, tick, like a perfect heartbeat from the stars. She stared at the pattern, then circled it with her pencil.

"This is odd," she murmured.

She checked again the next day — and there it was, still ticking exactly on time.

Jocelyn showed her supervisor, Professor Antony Hewish, who was surprised too. "It must be man-made," he guessed, maybe a radio signal from an aeroplane or satellite.

But when they searched the skies, they found no satellite there. The signal was coming from way beyond Earth. It was something no one had ever detected before.

For a while, the team jokingly called it "LGM-1" — short for "Little Green Men" — because they couldn't imagine what natural thing could make such a steady signal.

But Jocelyn didn't believe in aliens. She believed in data. She checked more charts, and soon she found another signal — and another, from different parts of the sky.

There weren't little green men everywhere. There was something new and powerful happening out there.

After months of study, scientists realised what Jocelyn had discovered: a pulsar — the remains of a massive star that had exploded long ago.

What was left was a tiny, super-dense core spinning incredibly fast, shooting out beams of energy like a lighthouse in space.

When that beam pointed toward Earth, radio antennas like Jocelyn's could "hear" its pulse — tick, tick, tick — across billions of kilometres.

It was one of the most important discoveries in modern astronomy, showing that even dead stars could still sing their stories through space.

Though her professor later won the Nobel Prize for the discovery, scientists around the world agreed: it was Jocelyn Bell's keen eyes and determination that made it possible.

Today, pulsars help us map the galaxy, track time more accurately than any clock, and even test theories about black holes.

MORAL OF THE STORY

Great discoveries often start as tiny details. If something looks odd, listen closely — it might just be the universe trying to say hello.

Epilogue

The Light We Carry Forward

When you turn off the lights at night, the stars above you still shine — even if you can't see them.

That's what curiosity is like. A quiet light that keeps glowing, even when no one is watching.

Every story in this book began with someone — or something—who looked at the world and said, "There's more here than meets the eye."

A girl saw a fossil and imagined giants beneath her feet.

A scientist listened to earthquakes and heard the Earth's song.

A teacher felt water and found a word that unlocked a mind.

An explorer mapped the sea and found a heartbeat under the waves.

An inventor listened to lightning and dreamed of light without wires.

All of them followed the same light — the one that flickers inside every curious mind.

That light is older than science, older than stories, older than us. It's the spark that made people look up at the sky and wonder why stars move.

It's the same spark that made them look down and find the bones of creatures long gone. It's the spark that makes you, right now, ask questions about the world and your place in it.

Some people think discovery is about having all the answers.

But the truth is — it's about asking better questions.

"Why does this happen?"

"What would happen if I tried?"

"What else could this be?"

Every question is a match. Every match can start a fire.

The scientists, artists, inventors, and dreamers you've met didn't all start with fancy tools or laboratories. Most began with a notebook, a thought, or a moment of wonder. They made mistakes. They failed. They tried again.

But they kept going because curiosity doesn't stop when it gets hard — it grows stronger.

That's what makes light special: it shines brightest in the dark.

So maybe your story is next. Maybe you'll find light in the way seeds grow, or how music makes you feel.

Maybe you'll wonder why the wind sounds different through trees than through streets. Maybe you'll build something no one has seen, or write something that helps people see more clearly.

Whatever it is, don't forget: the world is still full of mysteries waiting for someone just like you.

Because light isn't something we keep. It's something we carry — and pass on.

When Mary Ann Mantell drew a fossil, she passed her light to every palaeontologist who came after.

When Nikola Tesla spoke to lightning, his spark became the electricity that lights our homes.

When Marie Tharp mapped the ocean floor, she showed us that even hidden worlds can be drawn into view.

Every light connects — star to star, mind to mind, heart to heart.

And now, as you close this book, that same light rests in your hands. It may be small, but remember: every great fire begins with one spark.

So go on — wonder, question, explore, and share what you find. Keep the light alive.

And one day, someone else will see the world differently because of you.

THANK YOU

Thank you for joining me on this journey through the Amazing Stories For Sharp Minds.

For every story you read, every question you asked, and every spark of curiosity that flickered inside you — thank you. You are now part of the same light that guided all the dreamers, explorers, and inventors who came before us.

To the young readers who see magic in science and stories in the stars — never stop asking why.

To the teachers and parents who share books, build questions, and make curiosity feel safe — your patience lights more minds than you will ever know.

To the artists and scientists who remind us that beauty and truth are two sides of the same coin — your work keeps the world alive with colour and meaning.

And to every quiet dreamer reading this — your wonder matters. The world is waiting for the light only you can bring.

This book exists because curiosity exists — because every time someone chooses to learn instead of look away, the universe grows a little brighter.

So thank you, from my heart, for holding these stories, these people, and these truths close.

May they remind you that discovery never really ends — it just changes hands.

Keep your eyes open, your mind curious, and your light burning. Because the next great wonder might just begin with you.

With gratitude and joy,
Ali Hassan

REFERENCES

- Hidden Figures" by Margot Lee Shetterly — The inspiring true story of the women mathematicians who helped send astronauts into space.
- "Amazing Grace Hopper: Computer Pioneer" by Mary Gow — Biography of the woman who taught computers to understand language.
- "Tesla: Inventor of the Modern" by Richard Munson — A look at Nikola Tesla's experiments and imagination.
- "Marie Tharp: Mapping the Deep" by Hali Felt — The story of the woman who mapped the ocean floor.
- "Kristian Birkeland: The Aurora Explorer" — Norwegian Polar Institute archives and biographies.
- "The Lives of the Scientists" by Kathleen Krull — Engaging portraits of real scientists throughout history.
- National Geographic Kids — Articles and videos on fossils, volcanoes, oceans, and more.
- Smithsonian Institution Archives — Research on Mary Ann Mantell and early paleontology.
- United States Geological Survey (USGS) — Educational materials about earthquakes and the Earth's inner core.
- European Space Agency (ESA) & NASA History Division — Resources about William and Caroline Herschel's discoveries.
- "The Music of the Universe" by J. P. McEvoy — How astronomy and sound have shaped our understanding of the cosmos.
- Women in Science: 50 Fearless Pioneers Who Changed the World" by Rachel Ignotofsky — Illustrated stories of real trailblazers.
- "Curiosity: The Story of a Mars Rover" by Markus Motum — How curiosity drives exploration on Earth and beyond.
- National Geographic Kids Almanac — Annual updates on science, nature, and technology.
- "The Story of Science" Series by Joy Hakim — How curiosity built our modern world.
- Khan Academy Kids & NASA's Climate Kids — Free online tools to explore science through play and stories.
- "Science You Can Eat" by Stefan Gates — Fun experiments that explain everyday wonders.

NOTES

NOTES

NOTES

NOTES

Thank you for choosing and trusting us!

Don't forget to share your experience and give a review.

U.S.

UK

More Books For Sharp Minds

GEOGRAPHY FACTS for SHARP MINDS — FOR ALL AGES
ISBN
979-8396875029

ANIMAL FACTS — FOR ALL AGES
ISBN
978-1739511807

INTERESTING FACTS for SHARP MINDS — A FAMILY BOOK
ISBN
979-8374954661

GEOGRAPHY WORD SEARCH for SHARP KIDS
ISBN
979-8853389908

ANIMALS QUIZ BOOK for SHARP MINDS — FOR ALL AGES
ISBN
978-1739511814

ANIMALS QUIZ BOOK for SHARP KIDS
ISBN
978-1739511821

THE FASCINATING WORLD OF SNAKES FOR KIDS — Interesting Facts & Myths
ISBN
979-8377596882

ANIMALS WORD SEARCH for SHARP MINDS — FOR ALL AGES
ISBN
979-8856116716

THE FASCINATING WORLD OF DOGS — Interesting Facts & Myths about Dogs
ISBN
979-8379006990

THE FASCINATING WORLD OF CATS — Interesting Facts & Myths
ISBN
979-8387680601

ANIMALS WORD SEARCH for SHARP KIDS
ISBN
979-8856403212

HUMAN BODY FACTS SHARP MINDS — FOR ALL AGES
ISBN
978-1739511838

www.ingramcontent.com/pod-product-compliance
Lightning Source LLC
Chambersburg PA
CBHW072023040426
42447CB00009B/1704